Cocktails
And
Peacock Feathers

An Anthology of Poetry

Jane Barr

COCKTAILS AND PEACOCK FEATHERS

Jane Barr Books
www.Janebarrbooks.com

Cover and Book Design by Tymara Oberdries

Dedication

To the many women out there who wonder why they are still battling with all our contemporary systems which require them to think really hard about the care and management of their children in conjunction with the advancement of their careers and calling.

And to John, Jim and Pat Benson who once gave me a garret in which to work.

Table of Contents

1700 Hours

Before she pours herself a
Restorative gin. She wanders
Slippered on the manicured
Terraces of her home

Wintry London

Give me a ladder and I will
Touch the sky
I will scrub it clean with
Bleach

There is ice and the lights at four pm
Still in a stagnant fog

It does not stray
This grey, it does not go away

There is no sea, or sun, or stars

The city is wrapped up
In the veil of an old man's
Beard

Remembering Mansfield

We, us New Zealanders, call her our own
Would she have liked that?
Did she not belong to the world?
For she left our shores
To taste the life abroad
For that is what they called it then
Going abroad

He cello yawned and Katherine
Noted how her bow slid to and fro
Like icing some kind of fancy
Fairy cake. Her world
Would be filled, now, with
Observing

She flew from page to page
Sailing over her yellow desk and
Flying from her pain

Ampersand
Add to that
A dead baby
That was born in the faint breath of a
German spa. Grief is a salty wound

She fled to France, to the anon so that
She could gaze upon an azure sea.
So that she could dance on the coast
Of gaiety. So that she could dine, finely
On eggs and wine

Then later, later on
With gulps of air that barely brushed the membranes of
Her diseased lung and with her lips sporting little
droplets
Of red, red blood
She wept for her unspent life

She slept amongst those like her whose time was near
She despised the place so she ate only her words
And then like Elijah she climbed the varnished staircase
And over her right shoulder she called to one who loved
her

John, make sure, that you cook well my stories
Cook them up in a copper pot and make sure you
Actually burn them. She said

Up there I imagine her bowing and gliding
And dancing in a river of moonlight
There are urns of silver spoons and she sings
Oh so softly
For in her arms lies a babe

The Cat we Called Pie

She came in the dawn
Cold and wet. Piebald and tattered
One ear bleeding and a drizzly nose
She cried so we cared
Fed her fresh meat
And put out a yellow saucer
Of sweet warm milk
Susie wrapped her in a blanket as if
She was a doll and then she turned to me and said
What shall we call her?
Guy said call her Trouble
I said no. Susie said call her Cindy
I said no
In the afternoon the sun warmed her
And she curled up cute like a pie.
I said to my children we must take her back
To where Mum, to where?
To her home, we must find her home
Susie made up a bed in her doll's cot
And Guy made a leash for her
He had always wanted a dog
I drew in my very artistic way
Signs. I told my children to
Prepare themselves
Not one person replied to
My signs which I had taped
Carefully up on trees and notice boards
Pie cuddles into me
She is very often in Susie's lap or arms or snug in
Our old pram. Guy takes her for a walk on a leash
Made of string

A Writer's Nook

The desk is like a garden or so I pretend
Where ideas grow in its grainy top
At noon the leafy trees outside my window
Give shade and some kind of green soft shelter
In the eve, this place of swivel chair and lamplight
Becomes a cloak, a slipper
And my world is all words, etched on this kauri plain
And my thoughts are spilt in many pondering puddles
Poured from the copper coloured
Nib
Of an old marbled fountain pen
And the ink
Is radiant blue

A Gardeners Lament

The earth receives my madness and in turn responds
With orange in the roses and red in the plums

Tiny mirrors of love, of lemon and lace
Pinks, yellows and greens
Of beauty and grace

Absolution

Oh give yourself a break. I said. Give yourself some
credit
We are human. We fuck up all the time
Sketch yourself in soft pastels
Deck your shoulders in a bright shawl and find a
moment
In the last light of day to caress your broken heart
Stand in the shower and allow the silver shiny head
To rain down hard on you
Sit in the silt of silence and stretch out your palms onto
the calm floor
Attach yourself to the gravity of ground, to the place
called planet
For this is us. We fuck up, we fuck up. We make up
We stitch ourselves back together and we grow along
With some kind of wistful wisdom that holds us

Pinot Gris

Well the old girls like that one
The attendant said to me
What? I said back to him
Pinot Gris, the drop you are holding
Oh yes, my mother drinks this but so do I
And my friends too
I like it very much
Especially in a long stemmed grass
It smells of pear and oily hay
Did you know?

The old girls that buy it
Say they like that brand best
He said
I held the bottle against my
Breast as though I was feeding
A small child

My sweat lives in this 'ere bottle
I said to him and my tears too

He scanned the barcode
With his beep beep
And I rubbed my own label
A sketch of Joan of Arc
That I drew myself
This is my drop of gold I told him

And it goes well with oysters
And chicken and fish and

Figs and blue cheese

He didn't take any more notice
Of me. I knew that I had my own
Bags out in the storeroom somewhere
They had a fair headed Joan of Arc
Riding a black horse on them. Gold font

I held out the bottle for him
I gave it to him
He smiled, oh no, I am more of a beer man
And besides I shouldn't accept gifts
It's not a gift. I said

Si un Jour

Chores, glorious chores
Drive, mad lady, drive
In and out
The children clatter
Car door
Don't slam it
Slam

Next stop
Ballet shoes
And cricket bats
Cry, no sing me a river

Meal done
In slow cooker, cooking
That thing is indeed
My friend along with his
Mate. Rice cooker

Best friend though
Is coffee, coffee, coffee
And more coffee

So tired, so, so, tired
Oh to sleep. To dream
Of still waters and sanctuaries where
Women swim naked and flowers
Bloom eternally

God, why doesn't anyone listen
I told you, didn't I say
Pack your library books

Stop, red light, and another
Sing a song. Hum
Home to the sullen house
It mocks me with its dirty floors
And smeary windows

Night, here it comes
The children, I send them
To bed, a little too early

Then I climb into mine
The cat is on my duvet
Move, move you beast
I shout to him. He leaps off
And Adam's side is now
Empty, very empty

Where is Adam?
Adam my pilot
The man I married
Who promised he would
Never forsake me

He is delayed
Bad fog. Really bad fog

ANZAC MORNING

Tears salt my face
As the sun dawns this place
The solemn lines of soldiers crawl
And we bow our heads
In this dimmed glory
Where all grief is bespoke
A frost has bitten
Hands and toes
And rats have eaten woes
And those that fell
Were buried in minds
And hearts and fields
Long ago
We stand together
To prevent such horror happening again
But as humans, that seems it can never be
For the roll of the tide
Spurns not hope but ancient parody

Tiny Hands in Prayer

22

I, too, drowned in the English winter when my baby girl
stopped breathing
She was soft, so soft, like powdered silk
And she lay still on some ethereal silvered cloud
She woke, oh she woke, her white face turned sunny
She cried then on my shoulder. So close was she that our
tears merged. And melted on our cheeks. Our relief became a
mirror, shining on the grey
Metal like frame of the River Thames

Saturday Sport and Winter Mornings

Pregame
Fastened seatbelts
In the hush of the car
Clean crisp kit
Unmuddied footwear
Or bare feet for some
Jiggling knees
And nervous tummies
Some vomit, some do not

The court, the frosted field
Blades of grass in the white ice of winter
Or hard courts slippery from frozen dew
The sun beats down, the wind lashes
And the rain often comes to watch

The First Half
Merriment and sideliners with their paper cups
Of coffee, tea and hot sugared enthusiasm
Umbrellas up when the rain decides to
Join in the animated sting

Half time
The injured ones race on with drink bottles
In old milk bottle crates. The mothers old school
Come on with plastic containers of orange segments
The father's converse about the ref and coach and their own
Boy/Girl
It is a miscellany of tribes
But one small thing holds them all together. The rules
They must uphold for in this roguery the valued is yielded
The child becomes a citizen of the world

The Second Half
Tousled, sweat soaked hair and skin
Makes the kinder glisten in the halo
Of the rain that embraces them fully
One team has to win, that is the way
That is the custom
The ball is King

Full time
Rubicund faces. Some love that
It's over. Some do not
Some want to return next week
Those that do not- do it to please
Their elders
Those parents, the elder faction. That truly
Believe all scores are settled
With the toss of a coin
And the throw of a ball

The After Match
Mud from boots,
From feet, from fields
And wet from puddles and
Showers and the car is steamy
And the seatbelts are on
But now the driver stops
At the dairy and the players
Disembark. Pies, sausage rolls
Drinks and cream buns
For some that is all they play for
For some that is not the goal at all
For the treat is the solid silver
That lives in the dusty cabinets
Of the clubroom halls

Tea for Two

Sit with me and I will listen. I will not judge you at all
Drink me down, drink down my blessing
Now let that amber warmth go straight to your heart
Let it smooth out that scratch that swims in your soul
Let the tea bind you to life and tell you that you are
Loved
Loved by who? You say. Well the tea leaves make
clouds
They form stars and suns and flowers. They make a
World within a world

The Blue Room

The blue room that he slept in is empty
Like day with sun, blue and I are alike
We retreat and fade. We enter a background
And we splinter into pools of darkness

The light of blue comes in the palest forms
And then seeps into a midnight colour of deep dark ink

He said I am leaving. Good I said. Don't hold me
So he didn't. I said take your skin and my old woollen blanket
And leave

I sit on his side of the bed with the
Eternal blue of this room
I drink coffee
I eat cake

Napier Dressed Up

Deco, in the afternoon sun
February and the light sea rattles
On the pebbly shore

The town is painted
In pastels
And in the light of the eve
A fairy creeps mimicking the dance
Of a leftover time

The concrete echoes
The mourners thoughts
And the street is peopled
With lipstick red smiles
And braces, and boater hats
Blazers of stripes and dropped waist dresses

Dance the Charleston with me, take tea
With me and drink champagne
And toast a renaissance of
Class and Gatsby like dreams

The fountain cools with coloured rain
It lights a city renewed and all candy cane

And rising from the blueness
Of the Ocean Pacific, gentle as song
The waves beat upon the shore
And the gulls chant
And from the rounded bay a tune
Rises and stands on the corner of time

From Southampton, England to Christchurch, New Zealand 1867

From the port of my homeland to the edge of the world

We sail
And after this moist journey of stink and vomit
We disembark into a turbulent tide
Where my petticoat soils and rips on the idle driftwood
The air is solid blue
Salted from a recent storm
I search amongst the debris on this lonely beachhead
For something familiar but it is bare

There is not much joy here. I am writing to my family
But I tell them none of this. I do not tell them that it
aches
To write with my blistered and torn hands.
I tell them that the summer is nearly here
And it is good in this vale

My husband is quiet and solemn
He likes to take a drink
We use the coins my family donated
I do not tell them this
He becomes merry after his ale
And we take love but still no bairns
I do not write of this

I tell them that I miss them
And I tell them that our spring
Is moody. A gale blows quite

Strong

There is no turning back. I knew that when we left
I leave out the desire to go back home
I tell them in spidery inked words
That Reg and I are using their money
To build a new home, in this lovely new land

I post the letter the next day
I cry all the way home to our little hut
Reg doesn't like it when I cry
He tells me to wait, to be patient
And it'll come good. He promises me this
"You see," He says, "We had none land back there
But here in God's country we do. We have land Love,
We have land like the toffs."

The Turtle

Little turtle in ancient shell
Is puzzled by the fragments
Of shiny food, a feast that
Twists and turns in the murky deep
The truth lies hidden in sand
And surf
Then, then, too long
The realisation seeps out
Too long does some kind of negligent
Hope breed
Indifference and lethargy
It begins to ascend with the concerned
They protest
They voice, they fight, they
Demand. They march telling
The darkest tale of woe
They unleash earnest and wise words
Into a sea of the obtuse. They hark,
They plead, they shout into the
Ears of greed. They say they will not stop
Until they have turned around
The mess made by man's unkind hand
But the turtle cannot hear them. He finds
A twisty slither of what looks like smelt
He eats it, this morsel. But it doesn't
Taste as it should. It does not sit well
Within him. He writhes in pain and atop
The ocean blue he misses the cordial current
His eyes become dull. He is lost in an ache
So deep. He dies within a seaweed shroud
On the congested highway to hell

A Child Grows in Me

There is a babe inside of me
I wonder if he or she is lonely
My Grandmother tells me, that she,
For she knows apparently that she is
A she, is not lonely for dear she says
To me, she bathes in the holy waters

I'm a scientist and I consider this, as the speck
Inside my womb grows
Much like the embryo inside the egg in a nest
 I have a book
That shows me that it is the size now of a
Plum. A plum that swims in holy waters

I call it The Foetus or Feety. My Grandmother tuts
She is little Dot dear, little Dot
I had a sister called Dorothy dear did you know that?
I did know that
Dorothy is such a nice name she tells me

The Birth

I am too big
Too huge
Too uncomfortable

I had to finish work
I miss my white sterile office
Swishing test tubes and
Stirring beckers and
Sitting down on my high stool
To write up my notes

I am at home
Cast on the couch
I am tearful so I
Watch telly

I did not find out the sex
Didn't want to know

I phone the midwife
Demand to be induced
She says no, no
We must wait
Baby will come when ready

That night it starts
My mind slows
And sinks into a dream space
My friend, my birthing partner
Says I am too calm
She has four sprogs, so she knows
But then the cramps come fast
And I am not calm any longer

—

The midwife will meet us at
The hospital. I slug it out
And when I am in that room
The birthing room I shout and heave
I make indentations in my mate's arm
With my short fingernails

Walk around, the midwife says
Good for baby. We walk around
The midwife thinks we are a couple
That is okay

Now my down below
Feels like my nose did
When I was a kid and I got so sunburnt
That the skin peeled back
Right down to the bone

This pain is not possible
Breathe, breathe the pair
Of angels beside me say
Push, push hard, that's it
They coo

The midwife's hand
Has the head. She smiles that smile
Her hand like a dove over the wet hair
A little girl, she says. Congratulations
My friend cuts the cord
While I hold the child to my chest
There is a hush, so deep and vast
My soul kisses the child
Hello Dot I say

The Highlands

<u>The morning</u>
After the breakfast service and
After the pieces are made
I write out my thoughts in this brown heather madness
On this midge eaten day
Nervous. What will I cook?
My imposter's heart beats loud. I make the large curvy words
Print my mis-en-place in the graph lined book

<u>The Afternoon</u>
In that incessant dusty heat I catch a salmon
I gut it and fillet it. The Ghillie is amazed
My uncles fished. I know how I say

<u>Night</u>
In my own little wing
After dinner service I soak in a peat coloured bath

<u>The Dream Time</u>
Sleeping and reading
Waiting for my alarm to beep
As the tension fills my tummy
I dream an odd dream where
My chest is wrapped in bacon and I
Am soaked in wine and braised
In an ancient oven

<u>Before sunrise</u>
A sombre kind of sermon sings in my head
Of people long ago who walked these tan hills
And drank the tawny whisky

<u>Looking out my window</u>
Madness, stone buildings, a bothy, mountains and a
river

<u>Presenting for the day</u>
The help, I am the help, the servant
I am from strong mixed blood
But my roots, cast them down long enough
And they grow nearby

<u>Mid-morning coffee</u>
I wear chef whites monogramed with my own name
I stir the saucepans with a wooden spoon
And taste my creations with my own little spoon
Made of sheep horn. I stir up my DNA in my mind
Let it rest on the remnants of a family crest drawn
In this land

<u>Thirty days on</u>
London waits for me. I have clients
There and everywhere. On the overnight train
I play patience and drink scotch. But the lodge still
Haunts me. It has got inside me somehow. It once
Belonged to the Prince Regent. Royal DNA rests
On the bedframe in that little wing in which I slept
I button up my coat. It is cold in the sleeper.
I put on my woolly boots and smell the sheep of home

Remedies From Around the Rim of a Wineglass

That scary edge. That prickle in my stomach. That
doubt that needs to go
First sips. Joy

The office today was full, oh so full, of fractured egos.
Of bickering and snide remarks
What kind of life do I live? Dodging people so that they
will not hurt me

Well they are gone now. Out of sight, out of mind. The
sofa is my boat
And the red ruby liquid of a particularly charming
Pinot noir runs smooth down my throat

Behind my eyelids I pray for some kind of change
Some kind of luck
Athena, old girl I say. Pass me your shield and take the
oars
Row me to your island

Carthage

She has a suitcase locked for future reference
She wears thick black sticky mascara and tight leather
pants
Once she shined. Once she laughed. Once he showered
her with gifts and gave her flowers

But her trampled mind now rests in poverty
She does not sleep without pills
She rises uncluttered and takes one step forward and
two steps back
Her feet rides on a carpet of broken eggshells and
shattered glass

In the morning she leaves for the Nail Bar
She is good at filing, at manicuring
And amongst those oiled pink cuticles and
White mooned pinkies she allows herself to think
Of not the hard but the soft

She leaves that afternoon after work
For the refuge that her colleague spoke of
At the secret address she is welcomed without
Questions
They show her to room and she climbs into a nest
Of stale blankets
She shuts her eyes tight, tight
The tears try to escape, to run out of her
She thinks now of only a tent
What colour is it?
It is mauve and made of silk

A Madwoman's Pleasure

I take up my spade and I say to that spade that I love
him
And then arm and arm we dig and turn the sodden soil

And then I take Rosy the hose, a snake in disguise and
she hisses at me
And I hiss back at her and we water like God when
Noah was around

And then I take up the bucket. I bought her specially for
she was purple
I call her Hyacinth and I fill her with sheep shit and we
feed the hungry starving soil

And all of us, yes all of us are like inmates
Mad sun-seniled inmates
On an island in forty degrees

We sow, we till, we hoe, we plant, we pick. We stand
back and admire
The place we have created

And the twine in my hand ties me up like a parcel.
Kinky I say
Oh how I love this old game. The music of the leaves
The trees standing guard, the flowers with their
Coloured hats bobbing in the breeze

After The Rain

The darkness is numbing, deep and frozen
My eyes are blind and my ears are deaf
At last the hush of grief finds some sort of colour

Clear as morning light I see the picture that is painted
on my soul. The black and white and grey starts to
move

That picture, that photo, that painting
Used to cry and weep
But now on certain days it smiles

But
Am I allowed to put down my umbrella?
Am I allowed to feel okay?

Oh Crackly Radio

Old man radio still lives, still mutters
Once in the hands of the paternal gardener
Whose muddy hand prints are still on its robust
Leather jacket
And when the gardener painted, he did splatter globs of
White on its chest
Your voice, oh radio, only has one frequency. Yes just
one
The channel of sport. Rugby, cricket and racing
And on a sun-soaked afternoon, or on a dew filled
morning
Or as you suffered through a snap of southerly rain
You cheered, echoing the sounds of the spectators
You are a songbird of sorts, an endangered species
You sit beside the lawnmower and the chainsaw
In your wooden framed nest
And in your silent speckled vest with your hoarse
Kind of voice you are unseen
You are wise little old radio
For you bring knowledge in a stormy world
When the power is out and the rain pours thick
You come in handy, vital even
And then you return when the flood is done
To your pulpit in the church of all things
Sport and all things garden

Bucket and Spade

The
Grandfather surveys his kingdom
That is dripping with flowers and swimming in dew
The garden tap spits into a green watering can
Collecting water needed not wasted

The
Shed is papered with pages of old magazines
Makes for good reading when a strong cup of
Char is poured

The
Lines of lettuces, like fat green soldiers march in
The fertile well tilled soil
The raspberry canes are guards of honour and keep
The civilian strawberries safe

The
Grandchildren arrive in their dresses
They strip down to their singlets and undies
And they jump and skip in the sprinkler fountain
They talk of treasure and pirates and fairies

The
Grandfather turns away and shelters in
His green garden shed. He sips his thick tea
And reads about frogs in the Amazon

Ode to her Firebox

The fireplace, yes it was grand
Wide curved mouth of brick
Mantlepiece of fine kauri
Built with the hands of an old craftsman
But it needed a guard, all the time, to keep the
House safe and even then the woman could not go
Out in case a spark darted out and then came fire
The man came and installed what the woman of the
House called a crematorium. It did breathe warmth
Into the old bones of the house and the fear of fire and
destruction
Vanished
But was it worth it?
Trading great beauty for functionality?
She stacks now, the woman she stacks, like a Vestal
Virgin
Great mountains of firewood. She makes monuments
And great works of art to honour, to replace
The old hearth and mantel
That once lived in her home

Bird Shit on the Sheets

The trees wave like sails on a green sea
And the wind is whippy, sheet drying whippy
The laundry basket like a sea chest receives its fine
cargo
Great cottons and fine linens

I extract the pegs from my floral apron pocket
And the pegs stand straight up like dicky birds
On the wire line

Later that day I harvest the washing, never trust a night
And then my own ringed fingers fold the cloth in the
last of the sunlight as it falls in great waves on my old
Wooden table

Shit, one sheet, just one shit is shitted on
Bugger. I bundle it up and throw it in the
Washing machine
And before the piles of material origami
I nurse a gin in the heavenly scent of
The Clean and Folded

My Gran

Gran wore an old brooch attached to her blue suit
It was all marcasite and silver and shaped like a bow
Gran all secateurs and *Cyclax Milk of Roses*
That's how I remember her
She always wore a large brimmed hat
That made small square shadows upon
Her soft radiant face

The Warm Islands

The frosted islands appear over the great windshield of
the shuttle bus
The frothy waves are like lemonade, lucid, lucid and
lapping

I catch sight of my toe nails
Like shells in my flesh

The bay is mainly blue. Sinking at the sides into green
Grecian colours

I check in and lie down on the tied dyed bedspread. It is
cool and a fan above
Me whirs

On the balcony I am solo. Hannah Solo
The obstacles I faced were
Like Uluru. Like Mount Cook. Like Everest.
But I persevered. I needed
 To be wholly alone

The midnight sky is creamy. The moonlight is like rain.
The knots inside of
Me grow even tighter. They are deep within my skin
They start to turn to the colour of burnt sand

I sleep the sleep of Snow White
I doze and sleep again
Then in the aftermath of a light night
And in the piercing dawn I scrape my soul clean
I take my ashes out to the tide

I tidy my room
I put my things in neat ordered piles
It is beautiful, the simplicity of it all
The peeled layers of me disappear

I dress only in my dreams

Indigo

Deep blue, radiant blue, purple
It waltzes on lavender's silken shades
In the night sky it slips under a diamante moon
The stars that glaze the sky look up and see
A chandelier candled in amethyst

Soft Sand

Curl a toe inside its grains to feel
The heat of the day or the cold damp rain
Seaweed stew with a foamy creamer floats upon
The tides of time
Write in watery words in this speckle of ground glass
And then let them be erased, these fine words
As old sea skates gallantly
Across the sand

The Folly of being Human

The sauce, liquor, booze, piss, juice

My mind is gone
 I am swimming in a gel of imperfect particles
This drink does support my ragdoll being
Shickered, trolleyed, drunk, tipsy, I skid off to bed
In the morning I beat myself up
Bruising myself until I swear to never again
Do this. I won't take to the drink. I will not do this
Ever again
With two white tablets and a strong coffee
I go into work. Everything is fine, yes fine
No one knows, except Les who sits across the
Way from me. For at morning tea I purchase
A sausage roll
All good lass. He says
I nod
I have completed this morning what all those
Sitting near and around me can never do
Les reads me
He says in the softest of voices
The good world needs people
Like you

The Feline Dentist

She is cat like. That is how I describe her
But only to myself
She wears big tortoiseshell glasses
And she has green eyes lined with fine
Black
She wears orange lipstick

She does not like to use
A formal salutation
She is Verity, she says, I do teeth

She guides me to her chair which
Is upholstered in leopard print
She places a silk cushion at my back
And she says, softly, what music do you like?

I nod my head, shake it, indecisive
Shall I play Bach then? She purrs

With gloved fingers she examines my pearlies
She takes some X-rays and asks her assistant to take
Some notes on a white tablet. She speaks in cat code
I know it's bad. She smiles and makes me a drink
A kind of pink drink that I do not need to spit out
It is the same one I get with my massage
Down the road

She clicks her high heels and comes back with
A white shiny folder. The prints outs from the white
Tablet but in layman's terms

Long term care, she says. It's essential for
Overall health, not just oral health but all
Health, stomach, heart, liver etcetera

We have a payment plan. And an option to beautify
Your smile. Take your time and I will have Sissy call
you in a day or two to discuss options

She helps me out of that big cat chair
 I walk to my car and I read from the big white folder
For less than a cup of coffee a day………
I imagine my future. With bright white teeth
And a big healthy heart. Fresh breath etcetera, etcetera

The Big Fridge

Oh you big white monastic tomb
Whose chill prolongs life

Grateful, yes we are
For all the red set jelly
In your belly and the mushrooms
Cosy in their wrinkled skins

In the clear plastic coffins that
Lie in your girth we keep
Vegetables and cheese

Fill up my stomach you big
Brute.
I open your overcoat and close it
Just like my kids used to do

I pour some wine taken from your
Arm. I take a tomato, very cold
And cut it into slices on a white
Dinner plate. I arrange one
Large lettuce leaf beside it
And a little nudge of cheese
Bon apetit me

Cocktails and Peacock Feathers

I am in a vast room painted lemon
And in the far corner is a golden urn
Full of peacock feathers
A fan overhead spins and it sings
I never imagined I would sit in such a room
Let alone lounge on this couch of blue
I am very tired. Very tired
My yoga teacher tells me to breathe
Very deeply. It makes some racket when
I do this
Today though I take out a cigarette and stroll
To the small portico outside the very large
Room
I have not had a ciggy in thirty years
It is exquisite, truly exquisite
I have just the one
When I return to the sofa
On the southside of the room
I hail the waiter
"A martini" I say
I'll have two
Then I order coffee
Of which I have three
At four o'clock I walk out of
Those ivory corridors
I wait in the bus stop
For the 207
To take me home

—

1800 Hours

Honesty, truth, honesty
Take all of me
Take me most thorough
And deliberately
Wrap me in kindness
And with gentleness
Lace up my soul

To Follow

At the end of 2024 Jane is releasing her novel entitled "World".
It is about Andronicus who follows Alexander the Great as he sets out to conquer the world.
In his travels Andronicus meets the beautiful Roxane whom Alexander marries.
Like Odysseus before him Andronicus' path is long and taxing. Roxane remains composed throughout her life which is mapped by insurmountable struggle.

"What we would have given for the arid heat of Persepolis or the rough coastal plains as that northern bitter wind raged and waged war upon us. We struggled to find one tiny bit of comfort beneath the imposing Sogdian Rock. What I wouldn't have given then to have had that gold that had slept under the watchful gaze of the Fates." (Andronicus as he keeps wait under the Sogdian Rock)

Facebook @Janebarr
Instagram @Janebarrbooks
Website www.janebarrbooks.com